James Hautman

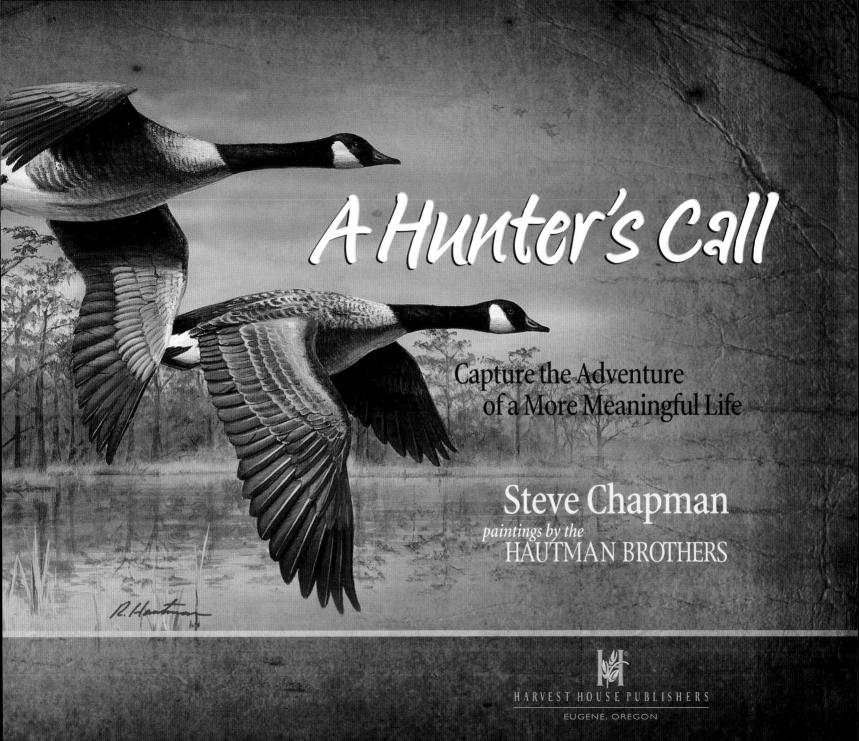

A Hunter's Call

Capture the Adventure
of a More Meaningful Life

Steve Chapman
paintings by the
HAUTMAN BROTHERS

HARVEST HOUSE PUBLISHERS
EUGENE, OREGON

A Hunter's Call
Text Copyright © 2005 by Steve Chapman
Published by Harvest House Publishers
Eugene, Oregon 97402

ISBN-13: 978-0-7369-1492-5
ISBN-10: 0-7369-1492-7

Artwork designs are reproduced under license from © 2005 by The Hautman
Brothers, courtesy of MHS Licensing, and may not be reproduced without permission.

Design and production by Koechel Peterson & Associates, Minneapolis, Minnesota

Scripture quotations are taken from the Holy Bible, New International Version®.
NIV®. Copyright © 1973, 1978, 1984 by the International Bible Society.
Used by permission of Zondervan. All rights reserved.

Portions of this book were excerpted from *A Hunter Sets His Sights* by Steve Chapman
(Harvest House Publishers, 2005).

Printed in Hong Kong

05 06 07 08 09 10 11 12 / NG / 10 9 8 7 6 5 4 3 2 1

A well established duck hunting blind is not just a place where gun powder
is expended and feathers flutter out of the sky to the frigid waters that surround it.
It is a kitchen where carbohydrates and fat do not matter,
a den where a family gathers to talk and laugh about past hunts,
a living room with walls filled with items
that trigger mental picture memories of missed hunters and dogs.
And, a duck blind is a bedroom where its temporary dwellers
rest their souls and dream of future hunts.
It's home. And I like going there.

STEVE CHAPMAN

> *"Everything that lives and moves will be food for you.*
> *Just as I gave you the green plants, I now give you everything"* (GENESIS 9:3)...
> *Hunting, therefore, is something that has been part of human life*
> *since the very beginning, and God gave it to us*
> *so that we could benefit from it and enjoy it.*
>
> JIM GRASSI

It Takes One to Hunt One!

THE WILD TURKEY was Benjamin Franklin's choice for the bird that would be recognized as one of our national symbols. Why he chose it as a nominee or why it never received that place of honor would be interesting to know. I'm sure one could dive into the archives and find out, but why do that when it's a lot more fun to guess?

Starting with the reasons for rejection, I can think of only two possibilities. One, it's just not the prettiest bird on the planet. With a face like that on our dollar bills and presidential emblems, it would be tough to look at them for very long and find patriotism welling up inside. The poor thing was not graced with handsomeness. The male, especially, got a serious whack in the kisser with the ugly stick. And to the die-hard lovers of the wild turkey, I'm sorry but that thing—that wattle—hanging off an old gobbler's face is really gross. I think they make medicine for that! I will admit though, from the neck down, it's a beautiful creature, which could be said of a lot of humans.

Second, the flight of a wild turkey does not match that of the final choice, the Bald Eagle. There's something about the high-flying ability of the eagle that stirs in us a desire to rise above things such as ignorance and poverty. It moves us deep in our hearts. On occasion the broad-breasted turkey must take to the air to escape danger, but they don't sail very far. Though pretty in flight as they leave the roost at daylight and whoosh overhead on their way to their kitchen table, they just can't get to the heights that an eagle can. Of course, if the eagle was packing enough food on its breast to feed a family of five, it too would have a hard time flapping its way into the stratosphere. The wings are there, the wind is waiting, but the

Don and Eddy talked me into going along... warning me that I would never be the same after the attempt— and they were right!

"pot breast" of a turkey gets in the way.

For whatever reason, you won't find the heavy, homely, and horrifically ugly face of a turkey on your silver dollar. Nor will it ever grace the banners that wave over this nation. The two birds in question have a lot to offer but the bottom line is that *flying* was chosen *over* food. And that's fine with me.

Regarding the possible reasons that Ben Franklin presented the turkey as a good representative of America's positive traits, there are a few that seem logical. Could it be that the turkey was initially considered because it was a plentiful food source for the people who lived here and for those who eventually settled on this continent? In my experience as a turkey hunter, there is a consistency about the breast meat that is both tender and tasty.

For people who fashioned their own arrows, turkey feathers for fletching were the best. The length and strength of its quill and the width of the plume added to the arrow's durability and accuracy of flight. Furthermore, arrow-making was more than the construction of a practical tool for hunting and self-defense. It was also a work of art. Turkey feathers were often used as vanes on the shaft because they held ample color and eye-catching marks. This was true then and remains so today.

Of all the reasons the wild turkey should have gotten the votes needed to occupy the office of "top bird," I can't help but wonder if Mr. Franklin's main reason for putting the *Meleagris gallopava* on the ballot was rooted in his love for hunting it. I have a feeling that after many frustrating attempts to harvest a turkey, he developed a level of respect for the bird that was similar to the amount of esteem others gave to him as a leading citizen of the nation. It seems reasonable to believe he had had some exciting encounters with the incredibly effective eyesight of a turkey. And it's conceivable that he had discovered how nearly impossible it is to see a bird that stays on the ground through the daytime, feeding beneath the underbrush well below eye level of the average-sized man. As far as I'm concerned, if Franklin's feelings about the turkey were grounded in his sincere regard for its illusiveness, that alone is good enough for me. I say it's not too late to call for another vote!

I admit there was a time when I didn't put turkey and deer hunting on the same line in terms of the excitement level involved. The reason was simple…I had never tried it. Then one day my friends Don Scurlock and Eddy Richey talked me into going along for a hunt during spring season in Tennessee. They warned me that I would never be the same after the attempt—and they were right!

That first hunt was unforgettable. Don and Eddy instructed me that two things were extremely important. One, camo cover for every part of the body was absolutely necessary. Don even covered his eyes. And, following his example, I shrouded my pump shotgun with camo tape. Without the proper concealment, there was no way to blend in with the surroundings and fool a turkey's highly sensitive peepers.

Second, they told me that when the bird is coming in, the slightest movement would likely spook it and send it scampering. The blink of an eye or a trigger finger sliding around to push the shotgun safety button had the potential to ruin the opportunity. I was cautioned that once a gobbler fixed on a hen call and decided to approach, my shooting position had to be already established, otherwise I would blow it.

There was enough exciting emotion in just the instructions Don and Eddy gave to cause my heart some considerable palpitations. I ventured on with them to the fields that morning on my first turkey hunt. As we walked on the dirt road well before daylight, we kept our talking to a whisper. Don had "put the birds to bed," meaning he watched them from a distance the evening before and knew where they had flown to roost. Knowing they were in the trees on a bluff nearby, we took care not to disturb their slumber.

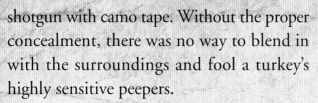

In the darkness, Eddy put two decoys out in the field, and then the three of us took our places along the tree line. Just after first light, Don began using a gift he possessed that is nothing less than remarkable. He had studied and practiced the wild turkey's language so well that he, with his man-made devices, could speak to them as if he were one of their own. With a light, dainty clucking sound, Don broke the morning silence. His "waking up" call initially got no response. But he knew what he was doing. He waited a minute or two and with the flat, waterproof mouth call made of tape and latex rubber, he spoke again. Behind us, a bird responded. I froze. Eddy was motionless. Don slowly looked over at me and though I couldn't see his face behind the mesh camo mask, I could tell he was smiling. It was the way he held his head that told me his heart was racing faster than the pistons in a screaming Indy car.

Suddenly, I heard my very first sound of the swish of turkey wings in flight as a bird sailed off the bluff and glided down into the field. The grace of its soaring was impressive. So was its size. I didn't realize how tall a wild turkey stood. I wouldn't have noticed had I not been crouched low against a big oak. From where I was sitting, the eyes of the hen that had landed in the meadow appeared to be looking down at me. It was an awesome sight.

I was already in the shooting posture and had been there since we sat down. I took the instruction about minimizing my movement very seriously and was trying to be a good student. The problem that arose was excruciating, however. After about 20 minutes in one position, my body started to protest. My derriere had lost its feeling and the numbness was creeping up my back and was on its way to my brain. But to move would have spelled disaster. Although my arms wanted desperately to shake, I forced myself to hold steady and hoped relief would come quickly.

Finally, a bearded bird descended into the field. The male is the only legal game allowed during the spring season, and the sight of one was welcome. As he landed near the hens, they briefly scattered. It was as if they were well aware that he came around only when he wanted "something." Except for this special time in a gobbler's life, when "love" is all they are after, they usually stay away from the females and travel in bachelor groups.

Finding himself around several attractive hens, the male began his ritualistic strutting. With his tail at full fan, his head changed colors from pale gray to a brilliant red, along with some white and a hue of blue. It was a sight to behold. The problem for the three of us sitting there waiting to send him to turkey heaven was that he was too far away. Don was careful not to talk too much with his calls for fear of saying the wrong thing and causing the gobbler to run off. All we could do was sit by and hope he meandered over within range.

Suddenly things started falling into place.

...that old bird might be ugly, but he's smart!

They were working their way around the field to where we sat. By then, the mixture of painful numbness and explosive excitement had started doing weird things to my entire body. Knowing I couldn't move, I wanted to shake like I had grabbed hold of a live electric wire. I was loving this new experience! In the stream of pure adrenaline that was rushing through my brain, I saw a reflection of the future. I could see all the seasons of springtimes yet to come, and I knew where I wanted to be when they arrived. I wanted to be at the edges of fields, tucked away in my camouflage among the leaves and branches, doing what I was doing at that very instant. Before I had ever pulled the trigger on one of these birds, I had become a bona fide, no-holds-barred turkey hunter. I had been "spurred."

As it turned out that morning, none of us were able to score. When the gobbler got within 50 yards, he saw something he didn't like and scampered off to another part of the farm in search of companionship. Sadly, the three of us gathered our decoys, seat pads, and wounded egos and headed home. But it was still exciting, and I have been on many successful turkey shoots since then. Every time it's a thrill.

Some final observations about the wily old gobbler…I have to admit I have a lot in common with him. For one thing, that old bird might be ugly (did I just insult myself?), but he's smart! And there's another thing that impresses me about him. It's in his nature to run at the very first sign of danger, and I have never seen him ignore that attitude. A mature male turkey is just that because he doesn't stay around for one extra second if he thinks his life or safety is in jeopardy. I've arrowed a lot of deer because they stood there a moment too long after detecting trouble. I got the best of their curiosity. Not so for a woods-wise gobbler. He's gone at the first hint of trouble. I deeply admire the gobbler's attitude of willingness to forego the next grub

worm, juicy bug, or even a fleeting, extra glance at the source of danger. He knows it's the key to his survival. I want to be like him. May I never forget that quickly running is the best way to steer clear of temptation.

With that worthy goal in mind, I will consider it a great compliment the next time spring season arrives in Tennessee and my sweet wife, Annie, looks at me in my boyish getup of head-to-toe camo and facetiously says, as she often does, "Turkey—it takes one to hunt one!"

Little Dog, Little Boy

STEVE CHAPMAN

Little dog, little boy
Billy Wayne called him Watchman Roy
Close as ice cream in a cone
Where Billy went Roy went along

Strong right arm
Broken stick
Billy threw it far
Roy brought it back
A simple game they both enjoyed
Little dog, little boy

And in the night when Billy dreamed
He had no fear of evil things
'Cause at his side was Watchman Roy
Little dog, little boy

Mama was mad 'cause Roy's paws
Left red clay mud on her kitchen walls
She grabbed a broom,
    tried to beat him like a drum
Billy laughs, Roy runs

Tall grass fields and a thousand trails
Spend a winter day chasing cottontails
When evening came
    he loved to tell his huntin' stories
Happy dog, tired boy

And in the night when Billy dreamed
He had no fear of evil things
'Cause at his side was Watchman Roy
Little dog, little boy

Now these are the tales my Grandma told
'Bout Grandpa Billy, her heart and soul
But today he went to find Ol' Roy
She said, "A little dog needs a little boy."

Now in the night when Billy dreams
He'll have no fear of evil things
'Cause at his side is Watchman Roy
Little dog, little boy

A dog teaches a boy fidelity, perseverance,
    and to turn around three times before lying down.
ROBERT BENCHLEY

He is your friend,
  your partner,
    your defender, your dog.
You are his life,
  his love, his leader.
He will be yours,
  faithful and true,
    to the last beat of his heart.
You owe it to him to be worthy
  of such devotion W

AUTHOR UNKNOWN

DOGS HAVE GIVEN US THEIR ABSOLUTE ALL.
WE ARE THE CENTER OF THEIR UNIVERSE, WE ARE THE
FOCUS OF THEIR LOVE AND FAITH AND TRUST. THEY
SERVE US IN RETURN FOR SCRAPS. IT IS WITHOUT A
DOUBT THE BEST DEAL MAN HAS EVER MADE.

ROGER CARAS

Of all the lessons a shooter will learn, this is the most important.

It doesn't matter if the target is a clay bird or a drake mallard.

Watch the target! Learn to trust your eyes.

Your hands and body will move the shotgun to where your eyes are looking.

Just make sure they're looking at your target.

GARY GOODPASTER & JIM ALEXANDER
"Shoot Better This Year"

*Successful hunters and fishermen are precise
observers of the world around them.
They have to be in order to be successful.*

GEORGE REITER

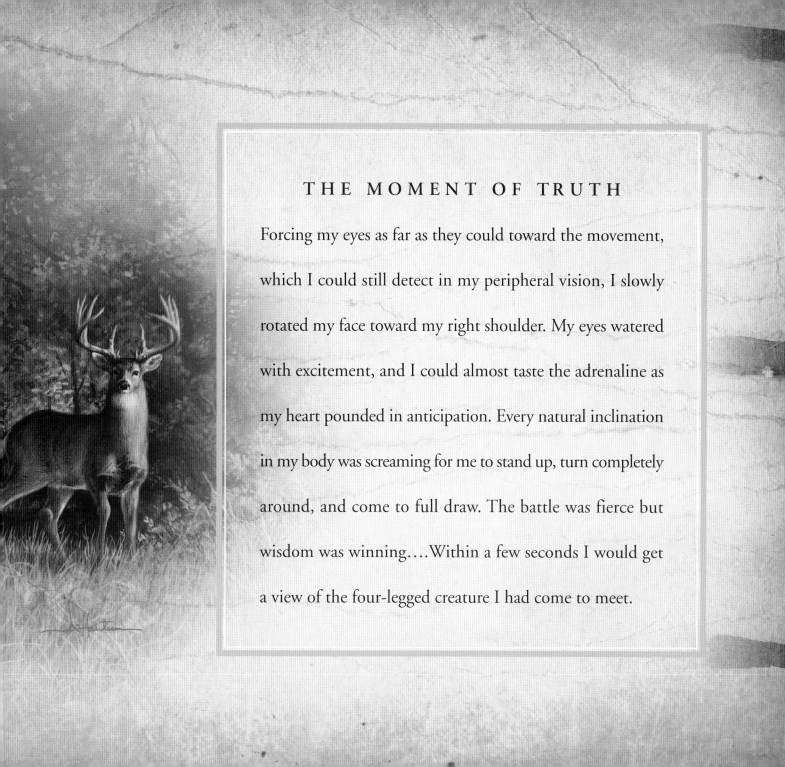

THE MOMENT OF TRUTH

Forcing my eyes as far as they could toward the movement, which I could still detect in my peripheral vision, I slowly rotated my face toward my right shoulder. My eyes watered with excitement, and I could almost taste the adrenaline as my heart pounded in anticipation. Every natural inclination in my body was screaming for me to stand up, turn completely around, and come to full draw. The battle was fierce but wisdom was winning....Within a few seconds I would get a view of the four-legged creature I had come to meet.

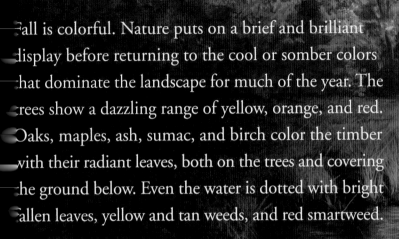

Fall is colorful. Nature puts on a brief and brilliant display before returning to the cool or somber colors that dominate the landscape for much of the year. The trees show a dazzling range of yellow, orange, and red. Oaks, maples, ash, sumac, and birch color the timber with their radiant leaves, both on the trees and covering the ground below. Even the water is dotted with bright fallen leaves, yellow and tan weeds, and red smartweed.

As the days grow shorter and frost forms on the lower areas of land, waterfowl start gathering together to begin their annual flight to their wintering areas farther south. Some species migrate by the calendar regardless of weather conditions. Others wait before moving south until water and food are no longer available. Diving ducks that find their food in the water are forced south as soon as the water freezes.

MAYNARD REECE

Just because it looks like a duck,
swims like a duck, and flies like a duck
doesn't mean it will come to any duck call.
To master all the music of the marsh,
you need a variety of calls
to make not just the quacks
of hen mallards but also the squeals,
whistles, peeps, and trills
of other species.

PHILIP BOURJAILY

James Hautman

It's great to get out in the woods and feel the wilderness around you,
but if you want to really feel where you came from, try outwitting the animals.
Try, on their own terms, to get close to a whitetail deer. It's a great high.
You'll never feel anything like it, without trying it for yourself.

RUSS CHASTAIN

The White Flag of Victory

MANY ARE THE TIMES I've been sneaking through a thicket, quiet as a mountain lion on the prowl, only to have my heart nearly burst through my sternum at the sound of an escaping herd of startled deer. In that moment filled with flying leaves, crashing limbs, and ear-piercing snorts, it's all I can do to keep from passing out.

While it's exciting to catch a glimpse of several of earth's most beautiful and illusive creatures, the sight of four or five or more whitetails bouncing away like superballs thrown on concrete is depressing. It's a sure sign that I would do well to just go on home. The chances of seeing the group again are about as good as getting to my treestand and finding Elvis sitting there in bell bottom camo pants.

I suppose there have been a few of us who've thrown an open-sighted rifle to the shoulder and managed to connect with a fast, escaping deer. Of course, the wisdom of that kind of shot is as little as the safety of it. In no way do I recommend spraying lead projectiles into the forest without knowing what is beyond the target. That's just not a smart thing to do. And even though I know it's unsafe and a low-percentage shot, when the whitetails suddenly fill my vision I instinctively try to get one in my sights. Though I never squeeze the trigger, unless one of them stops for a second and gives me a chance to look beyond his position, I realize it is an instinctive reaction that is nearly uncontrollable.

In regards to the "flagging" a whitetail deer does when running away, I can't help but wonder why our Creator chose to equip them with such opposing characteristics. On one hoof, deer are incredibly cautious. On the other, they are made highly visible because of the brilliant white fur under their tail. Since it is likely that none of us will fully know His mind on this matter (until we can ask Him personally), we are left to speculate on the reasons.

In no way do I recommend spraying lead projectiles into the forest without knowing what is beyond the target.

Interestingly enough, all the arguments I have heard hold so much logic that it seems each one could be true. Here's a sampling:

1. Throwing up the tail and revealing a mass of bright white tends to momentarily startle and stall a would-be predator. Once safely ahead of whatever might be chasing it, the deer will then often stop, drop its tail, and disappear by blending into its surroundings.

2. Deer in groups speak a silent language to each other with their tails. A flicker while grazing means they are relaxed. A slow rise indicates a warning to other deer that danger has been detected. A cunning hunter will

watch for these signs as deer are moving into his area.

3. The younger of the herd can more easily follow their parents or other adults, especially when a running escape is being made.

While I appreciate the common sense in all the above opinions, it will be fine with me if this unique trait of the whitetail continues as a mystery. Though it is likely to remain an unknown, one thing is for certain, when a hunter sees a snow colored, furry ensign bounding off in the distance, it's pretty sure that the deer prevails and the hunter's tag stays in his or her pocket. It may be true for battles between humans that a raised white flag means surrender, but not so for deer. For them, it's their way of saying, "We win!"

Choose one person to call the shots, and
trust his or her judgment. Among friends,
take turns taking charge so that each hunter
develops a feel for the right time to unleash
the guns. Appointing a designated shot caller discourages
the quick-draw artist in the group and assures that friends
all get the same opportunities for clean, close shots.

DOUG PIKE

GRILLED DUCK BREAST SALAD

Lindsey Williams

1 cup pecans, chopped
2 tablespoons butter
1 head romaine lettuce, washed, broken into pieces
1 cup sweetened, dried cranberries or Craisans
3 to 4 duck breasts that have marinated overnight in:
   ¾ cup bottled Italian dressing
   ¼ cup Dale's seasoning
1 cup sweet and sour dressing

Mix together Italian dressing and Dale's seasoning. Pour over duck breasts and marinate, covered, overnight in refrigerator.

Grill duck breasts over medium hot fire about 4 minutes per side. Do not overcook. Duck should be a little pink in the center. Chill.

Thinly slice duck breast and set aside.

Toast pecans in butter in a skillet on top of the stove. Allow to cool on paper towels.

Toss together lettuce, cranberries, and pecans. Lay several slices of grilled duck on top of greens. Pour sweet and sour dressing over all and serve.

SWEET AND SOUR DRESSING

1 cup vegetable oil
1 cup sugar
½ cup wine vinegar
3 teaspoons soy sauce
salt and pepper to taste
Blend all ingredients. Makes 2½ cups.
This can also be served over Foccacia bread with caramelized onions.

BASIC QUACK

As easy as it sounds, some callers never master a basic quack,

and then wonder why the ducks don't come into their spread.

Todd Heidelberger also stresses the importance of learning to end

the quack. "One of the first things my grandfather taught me was

to end my quacks. People use 'qua qua qua' when there needs to

be a clean, crisp, 'quack' instead. Stick to the basics and end

your quacks, and everything else is second."

www.duck.org

After more than 30 years of experimenting with different decoy spread configurations, Russell Caldwell has devised a rig that he has found to be most productive under a wide variety of conditions. "We place our decoys in tight bunches of about 25 each, which are much more visible to waterfowl from a distance than decoys scattered more widely apart," he says. "We leave a hole about 20 yards wide in front of the blind to provide the birds with a clear place to land, and we set several dozen super magnum mallards and a few motion decoys on the edges of the landing zone as an added enticement. For geese, we set a separate group of 100 hand-painted Canada goose decoys in a horseshoe pattern off to one side of the main decoy spread."

www.duck.org

Distances to incoming ducks and geese can be deceiving.
A foggy morning typically makes waterfowl appear farther away
than they are, and a bluebird day can make them seem closer.
Squinting from under a cap can also lead you astray, as can a
stiff wind. A good way to avoid shooting at out-of-range birds
is to place the farthest decoys at 35 to 40 yards out,
for an accurate marker by which to start guns.

DOUG PIKE

Six birds split from the larger flock and began their dance above our decoys. They feigned a retreat, then returned more committed. We were persistent and masterly in our calling. They started to drop, wings cupped. We sat up—out of nowhere—and the giant Canadas couldn't back-peddle fast enough. Bang! Bang! Bang! Thud, thud, thud. Bang! Bang! Thud, thud. One more—Bang! Thud. Perfect.

JOHN TARANTO

IN A CIVILIZED AND CULTIVATED COUNTRY, WILD ANIMALS ONLY CONTINUE TO EXIST AT ALL WHEN PRESERVED BY SPORTSMEN. THE EXCELLENT PEOPLE WHO PROTEST AGAINST ALL HUNTING AND CONSIDER SPORTSMEN AS ENEMIES OF WILDLIFE ARE IGNORANT OF THE FACT THAT IN REALITY THE GENUINE SPORTSMAN IS, BY ALL ODDS, THE MOST IMPORTANT FACTOR IN KEEPING THE LARGER AND MORE VALUABLE WILD CREATURES FROM TOTAL EXTERMINATION.　❧　PRESIDENT THEODORE ROOSEVELT

Hunting is not merely an acquired taste; the instinct
that finds delight in the sight and pursuit of game
is bred into the very fiber of this race (man). We are
dealing, therefore, with something that lies very deep.
Some can live without opportunity for this exercise
and control of the hunting instinct, just as I suppose
some can live without work, play, love, business, or
other vital adventures. But in these days we regard
such deprivations as unsocial. Opportunity for exercise
of all the normal instincts has come to be regarded
more and more as an inalienable right.
ALDO LEOPOLD

Like a dog, he hunts in dreams.
LORD ALFRED TENNYSON

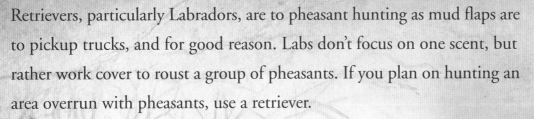

Retrievers, particularly Labradors, are to pheasant hunting as mud flaps are to pickup trucks, and for good reason. Labs don't focus on one scent, but rather work cover to roust a group of pheasants. If you plan on hunting an area overrun with pheasants, use a retriever.

MARK KAYSER

Dogs are our link to paradise. They don't know evil or jealousy or discontent. To sit with a dog on a hillside on a glorious afternoon is to be back in Eden, where doing nothing was not boring—it was peace.

MILAN KUNDERA

Late season pheasant hunting requires a different approach from that of early-season hunts. There are fewer hunters afield, but by the time the snow flies, most of the dumb birds are gone.... The survivors are seasoned and savvy. If a hunter doesn't plan his hunting approaches carefully, he might as well stay at home and put up Christmas lights.

MARK KAYSER

THERE'S SOMETHING SPECIAL, EVEN GENTLEMANLY, ABOUT A RING-NECKED PHEASANT HUNT. AT BEST, IT'S A WALK THROUGH THE FIERY AUTUMN UPLANDS WITH A FINE DOG, A SPECIAL SHOTGUN, AND AN OLD FRIEND OR TWO. IT CAN BE AS REFINED AS THE SOLID POINT OF A STATUESQUE SETTER, AS WILD AND FRANTIC AS THE HARD FLUSH OF A SCENT-CRAZED SPANIEL, OR AS CALM AND ORDERLY AS THE RUSH OF A SEASONED LAB. AND YOU NEVER REALLY KNOW HOW THE HUNT WILL GO UNTIL IT'S OVER.

STEVE GALEA

Nathan's First Turkey

THE MORNING WAS SLOW in terms of action. After sitting and "calling" in one place for about two hours with no results, my son, Nathan, and I decided to group up with my son-in-law, Emmitt. The three of us would walk and "talk turkey" with my loud box-call. The game plan was to skirt the field edges and about every hundred yards stop and send out an inviting call of a love-sick hen. Our hope was to connect with an amorous tom that might be hiding back in the timber.

Within 30 minutes, while the three of us slipped along single file at the edge of a narrow field, the connection was made. A mere 50 yards away, just over the crest of the hill and out of sight to our left, an old male turkey responded with a gobble that rattled the earth.

Emmitt had some previous experience with the sudden shock of a gobbling turkey, so he knew what to do. He quickly hid himself in the brush, sat down to reduce his silhouette, and rested his shotgun up on his knee, ready to shoot. Nathan, however, having never been close to a huge bird and having never been suddenly shaken by its boisterous call, froze at the sound of the bird's big voice. He was paralyzed by the unknown.

Realizing he had no idea what to do, I grabbed my stunned son by his belt and pulled him into the brush. I quickly pointed out a tree for him to lean against, instructed him to sit down and point his gun into the field with his finger on the safety button. A mere minute or so later, the brilliant white head of the frisky gobbler appeared in the tall grass about 40 yards away. I quietly whispered (as I thankfully filmed the entire scene), "Whenever you have a shot, take him!" *Boom!* The deal was done.

Emmitt and I had a good chuckle at one of Nathan's comments as we drove home. He admitted, "Dad, I thought at first that this turkey hunting was sort of boring. Sitting for so long with no action, then walking around making weird sounds with a wooden box. It all seemed fruitless…until… until…" and he smiled big as he continued, "I heard that bird let go its gobble. I thought my heart was going to jump out of my chest. He was so close, so loud, and so imposing when he came out of the woods at full strut." Then Nathan said the words I hoped to hear. "Dad, I'm hooked. I definitely want to go again!"

> *The game plan was to skirt the field edges and about every hundred yards stop and send out an inviting call of a love-sick hen.*

While our turkey hunt had a wonderfully rewarding outcome in that I now add spring turkey season to the time I can spend with my son in the field, something else resulted that is just as great. The three of us saw an encouraging truth hidden in the hunt. There are times in a person's life when, just like the instant Nathan heard the gobbler's intimidating voice and froze, he or she will feel paralyzed by inexperience. A new position at a job, for example, that requires a person to stretch their skill level or perhaps buying a first house. Or, though never having faced such an audience, agreeing to teach the children's Sunday school class at church.

When we suddenly face the unknown, we need guidance. We need someone who's been there before to grab us by the belt, so to speak, and pull us into cover and show us the next move to make. And just as Nathan was willing to follow the instruction he was given at that narrow field edge, we would all do well to embrace the life-giving wisdom from those who have already "been down the road." Whether God speaks to us through the people in our lives or talks to us directly through His Word or the Holy Spirit, it is important that we heed His wisdom and put to use the insights He gives us.

The sound of these thousands of geese honking and flapping makes a roar like the crowd cheering a touchdown at the Super Bowl. Then the geese settle back down on the lake. Still more birds arrive all afternoon. The sun sets and against the evening sky, slightly lighter than the black earth below, dark shadows of geese are passing overhead so close you can almost touch them. Their forms vanish into the darkness, but their noise continues. Back at home you drop off to sleep, the roar of thousands of honking geese still sounding in your dreams.

MAYNARD REECE

Canada geese are careful about landing in a spot that might contain danger, preferring the unlimited visibility of open country. But Canadas may drop into a small area of water to drink, feed, and rest, and once the first group is safely on the water, the next flock will readily approach and land without suspicion.

MAYNARD REECE

When one is hunting, the air has another, more exquisite feel as it glides over the skin or enters the lungs, the rocks acquire a more expressive physiognomy and the vegetation becomes loaded with meaning. But all this is due to the fact that the hunter feels tied through the earth to the animal he pursues. ...And the hunter begins to behave like the game, he will instinctively shrink from being seen, he will avoid all noise while traveling with the animal's peculiar attention to detail. This is what I call being within the countryside.

JOSE ORTEGA Y GUSSET
Meditations on Hunting

He Walked Here

IN MY EXPERIENCE the overall taste of doe is generally better. Early archery season males can be less "gamey," but after an old buck has been whipped by the rut and is drenched with the hormones that drive him crazy, it requires far too much extra spice to cover the wild taste. If the goal is to see the smiles on the faces of family and friends as they sit with their feet under my supper table and take in the animal I worked hard at harvesting, then bringing home an antlered deer can be risky.

The virtue of going antler-less is a message I have preached for years. When I see the covers of hunting magazines that exclusively feature the trophy bucks and their rocking-chair-sized antlers, I wonder if the over-emphasis on big, bruiser bucks furthers the notion that a doe is not worthy of our time and skills as hunters. Some hunters may feel less than accepted and successful if they fail to connect with an antlered deer. The harmful result can be that far too many spikes that would have grown to be well-endowed adults are killed merely for the sake of saying, "I got a buck!"

These are the feelings I strongly held onto. Then one day something took place that fiercely tampered with my convictions. I confess that I was sorely tempted to retire from the pulpit where I sermonized about the erroneous doctrine of "rack worship." What happened? *I saw him!*

I took my son, Nathan, who was home from college, to a stand I had prepared along the edge of a massive, cut soybean field. He faced south, and I was just across a small creek facing north watching a smaller meadow. I was not toting a weapon since my goal was to help Nathan fill a tag. The wind was

blowing across us, and the sun was peeking over the horizon.

Suddenly, 100 yards to my right in the openness of the field I was monitoring, I saw a deer approaching that I can only describe as…uh…well…diabolical. If my belief that hunting primarily for meat was a virtue, then I sinned—and did it big time! This buck's body seemed twice the size of any of the three "slick heads" I had already sent to the processor. And atop his head was the most beautiful, perfect set of antlers I had seen in a long, long time. They must have boasted at least a total of ten points. His gait was confident and majestic.

I whistled softly to Nathan to sneak across the creek and join me. The buck, without knowing we were nearby, turned 90 degrees and headed toward the timber on the far side of the field. Nathan arrived at my side just in time to scope the heavy deer and get a fleeting glimpse of its head gear. All the while

I had him in my binoculars, and I must admit that my heart had nearly stopped.

The massive and obviously dominant buck disappeared into the high grass and brushy edge of the woods. The two of us, still shaking, sat motionless, hoping he would reappear further down the field. After about 30 minutes of wishful waiting, we resigned ourselves to the likelihood that he was gone for good.

I had hunted that farm for several years and had not seen this size of deer. I'm not sure where he came from, but his arrival spelled trouble for me. For the rest of the season I became a…forgive me… rack hunter. My tightly wound philosophy about being mostly a food hunter came completely unraveled by the sight of the stately creature. My nights were filled with dreams about him. The days when I couldn't sit somewhere on that farm and watch for him were hard to endure. I longed to just

If my belief that hunting primarily for meat was a virtue, then I sinned— and did it big time!

get a glimpse of him again.

I discovered the many signs he left behind. His "scrapes" were broad and the licking branches were high. His rubs destroyed some young cedar trees that were well beyond sapling stage. The does in the area seemed extra skittish, and the young males were a bit more nervous. But of everything that revealed the big buck's presence, his hoof prints were the most telltale evidence of his enormous stature. They were deep and wide. The sight of his tracks alone did more to lead this meat hunter astray than any other of the markings that bore witness to his existence. I memorized them. I studied them. And I wanted him!

One day as I walked beside a line he had taken from one side of a plowed field to the other, probably the night before, the thought came to my mind, *He walked here!* The mystique of being on the very ground that the great beast had occupied just hours before

...there are signs on this great planet that provide proof that God has been, and is, among us.

was overwhelming. I stopped and dropped to my knees in the dirt. I spread my index and middle fingers apart about two-and-a-half inches and slipped them down into the depression left by the buck, and said again, "He walked here!" I was mesmerized by the connection I felt to that deer. It was a sobering moment.

As I remained in a kneeling position and took in the size of the tracks, I suddenly had one of those thoughts that cross not just the mind, but the heart as well. "Just as these prints testify to the presence of that majestic buck on the earth, there are signs on this great planet that provide proof that God has been, and is, among us. I whispered the revelation audibly but softly. "*He* walked here!"

I began to think of the deep and impressive tracks He had left to reveal His presence. I thought of the children He had given to my wife Annie and me. I was there in the delivery

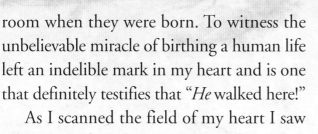

room when they were born. To witness the unbelievable miracle of birthing a human life left an indelible mark in my heart and is one that definitely testifies that "*He* walked here!"

As I scanned the field of my heart I saw other signs of His having passed by. The times when danger barely missed me or when I was filled with joy at being alive and being loved. *"God walked here!"* The phrase kept echoing in my head as I stood and looked toward the timber. I peered at the edge of the field for a moment then lifted my eyes toward the sky. The words floated freely toward heaven. "Thank You, Father, for reminding me through the big buck that roams in this territory and whose tracks I stand beside, that because of the signs You have left in my life, I can assuredly say to others, 'You walked here!'"

MY OLD HUNTING HAT

Someone once said, "I don't believe in luck…but I do believe in my old huntin' shirt!" Now I don't embrace the idea of depending on a charm, but I do have a severely tattered hat that I have worn for years. For some strange reason I feel better when I'm hunting under it. It's ugly and floppy and the camo pattern has nearly faded to the color of raw cotton. Still, I choose its cover above all other lids I own.

I suppose the real reason I prefer my old hat is simply because we have been many miles together, and it has served me well. It has absorbed my sweat during long stalks for deer, shaded my eyes against the brilliant rising sun while scanning the horizon for incoming mallards, and offered a warming shield against bitter cold winds that accompany winter days in pheasant fields.

Someday I'll be forced to retire my aging fedora. When that time comes, I will not toss it into a trash bin. Instead, with permission from my wife, it will find its resting place in our hallway curio where other valuable treasures are stored—a place of honor for a true friend.

I pray that my life will be meaningful to people just like my old hat has been to me. Comfortable, warming, protecting, absorbing, available, and enduring. And when my time is finished, I would be honored to be stored away in their hearts where they keep fond memories.

Walking up grouse without a dog is a subtle game of position and tempo.

Stealth is key. Wear quiet clothing. Don't bust brush unless rain or snow

has birds holding exceptionally tight. Slip quietly along brush edges,

fire lanes, and logging roads. Utilize deer trails and other natural breaks....

Early morning is prime time to catch birds sunning and feeding on trails.

RICH OSTHOFF

HAUTMAN BROTHERS

C O L L E C T I O N